A H‹

Novenas to the Saints

by Glynn MacNiven-Johnston
& Raymond Edwards

*All booklets are published thanks to the
generous support of the members of the
Catholic Truth Society*

CATHOLIC TRUTH SOCIETY
PUBLISHERS TO THE HOLY SEE

CONTENTS

What is a Novena? 4

How to use this booklet 6

January

St Thomas Aquinas (January 28th) 8

February

St Josephine Bakhita (February 8th) 11

March

St David (March 1st) 14

St John of God (March 8th) 15

St Patrick (March 17th) 18

St Joseph (March 19th; May 1st) 19

St Benedict (March 21st; July 11th) 22

April

St George (April 23rd) 25

May

St Peregrine (May 1st) 27

The English Martyrs (May 4th) 29

St Damien of Molokai (May 10th) 32

St Dymphna (May 15th) 35

St Rita (May 22nd) 38

June

St Anthony of Padua (June 13th) 41

St Thomas More (June 22nd) 44

St John Fisher (June 22nd) 47

July

St Christopher (July 25th) 49

St Anne (July 26th) 50

St Martha (July 29th)..53

August

St Teresa Benedicta of the Cross (Edith Stein) (August 9th)..........56

St Maximilian Kolbe (August 14th)..57

St Helena (August 18th)..60

St Monica (August 27th) 63

September

St Pio of Pietrelcina (Padre Pio) (September 23rd)........................64

St Joseph of Cupertino (September 18th) 67

St Raphael (September 29th)..70

October

St Thérèse of Lisieux (October 1st) 74

St Gerard Majella (October 16th)..77

St Jude (October 28th)..79

November

St Martin de Porres (November 3rd)...82

St Andrew (November 30th)..85

December

Blessed Charles de Foucauld (December 1st)..................................86

What is a Novena?

A novena is a way of praying, often for a particular need or grace. It consists of a prayer or prayers said over nine days. The word novena is originally Latin, and means "ninth" (in full, *novena dies*, "ninth day"[1]). This is because a novena lasts for nine consecutive days; on each day, there is a particular prayer to be said, or devotional practice to be made.

The original novena, the model for all the rest, is the nine days between Christ's Ascension and the descent of the Holy Spirit at Pentecost, when, as we read in the Acts of the Apostles, "all these [Apostles] joined in continuous prayer, together with several women, including Mary the mother of Jesus"[2]. The Church still asks Christians to pray with particular intensity between these two feast days for the Holy Spirit to renew the Christian community.[3]

There are many different sorts of novena; you can make a novena, perhaps to ask the intercession of a particular saint, using any prayer you want: the main thing is to pray it

---

[1] Although the official Latin equivalent is *novendialis prex*, "nine days' prayer".
[2] Acts 1.14 (JB).
[3] In 1897 Pope Leo XIII asked that this practice, which was of long custom, should be celebrated by all Catholics worldwide. The official *Handbook of Indulgences* states that "a *partial indulgence* is granted the Christian faithful who devoutly take part in a publicly celebrated novena before the solemnity of Christmas, Pentecost, or the Immaculate Conception of the Blessed Virgin Mary" (3rd edition 1986, English edition 1991, par.33 (p.72 in the edition published by the Catholic Book Publishing Corporation of New York)).

regularly for nine days in a row. Nevertheless most people will make a novena using a prayer composed for the purpose. Some novena prayers are long, and may include litanies, or meditations; others are short. You can make a novena using the same prayer nine times, or nine different prayers, one for each day. There are no rules; what follows are only suggestions.

The novena prayers in this booklet are addressed to individual saints, asking their intercession for whatever our intention may be. As well as interceding (praying) on our behalf, the saints are also examples of how the Christian life has been lived. Each saint experienced different events, and responded to them in different ways; we can see in their lives examples of how embracing God's will for us, whatever our individual circumstances, always brings the grace and strength from God we need to do what he asks us. To use religious language, the saints are examples of particular virtues. In the novena prayers that follow here, we have tried for each day to take one particular virtue or quality that a saint has shown, and ask God to make it our own too, according to our needs and circumstances, and in this context to make our prayer for any particular intention we may have, whether for ourselves or for another.

How to use this booklet

On each day of the novena, say the short prayer for that day, and add your intention (if any); then say the Our Father, the Hail Mary, and the Glory Be. Do this on each of the nine days.

Some of the novenas have only one prayer, which you should say each day for the nine days.

Some novena prayers ask for particular needs (consolation in grief, or thanksgiving); others, like those in this booklet, ask the prayers of a particular saint. The tradition and experience of the Church is that certain saints are especially powerful intercessors in a particular area, or for a particular need (St Anthony for things that have been lost, or St Gerard Majella for motherhood, for instance). We have given some brief indication of these areas at the start of each novena. This may sound like superstition, but in fact it is founded on the long experience of praying Christians. For some reason, which is sometimes obvious, but sometimes not, some saints are especially helpful for some types of need or intention. We should not be ashamed to have a devotion to a particular saint who has helped us or others with their prayers; after all, praying for each other, and for the world, is an especial charism and duty of the Christian, and one that (surely) does not end when we die. The saints have passed to a life that is fuller and richer than ours is now, or theirs was during their time on earth, and so we may rely on their prayers more than on our own; and there is surely no mystery if, after death as in this life, they, like us, have fields of particular interest or expertise.

Often people will start a novena eight days before a saint's feast day, so the last day of the prayer falls on the feast itself: so you might begin a novena to St Joseph on March 11th so as finish on his feast day, March 19th. You could also start a day earlier to finish on the eve, or vigil, of the feast. The dates of feast days are given at the start of each novena. But, again, there are no hard and fast rules here; you can make a novena whenever you want.

Note

These novena prayers have for the most part been newly composed for this booklet. Some of them are based on traditional prayers; this is generally mentioned in the text. Please note that none of these prayers has any official liturgical authorization; they are intended for private use only. The novena prayers are arranged in the order that their respective saints' feast days appear in the calendar.

Novena to St Thomas Aquinas

Feast Day: January 28th

A famous theologian, Thomas Aquinas (his surname means "from Aquino", his birthplace) was the son of an Italian nobleman. He became a member of the Dominican Order (Order of Preachers), and died in 1274 aged about fifty. Although he seemed a slow learner at first (he was fat, and habitually silent, and so was nicknamed the "dumb ox"), his teachers eventually realized he was an enormously talented theologian; he was also a man of deep prayer. He is best known for his voluminous writings, which include theological works, commentaries on Scripture, and some well-known prayers and hymns. His most famous work is the *Summa Theologiae* (Compendium of Theology), a systematic treatise covering the whole of Christian theology, which was a standard textbook until the 1960s. He was declared a Doctor of the Church in 1567. He is often considered a patron saint of study, and of education in general.

First Day: You experienced the mockery and mis-understanding of others; teach us to bear with patience, as you did, those times we receive the scorn or ridicule of others. We pray especially for [*add your intention*]. *Our Father – Hail Mary – Glory Be*

Second Day: Those who noticed only your body were surprised to learn of the great knowledge of and love for God it concealed; help us not to judge others by outward appearance, but to remember that all men and women are made in God's image and likeness. We pray especially for [*add your intention*]. *Our Father – Hail Mary – Glory Be*

Third Day: You had a great knowledge of and love for the Scriptures; help us to hear God's Word and respond to it as you did. We pray especially for [*add your intention*]. *Our Father – Hail Mary – Glory Be*

Fourth Day: You had a profound love for Christ in the Eucharist; help us, too, to experience this same reverence and love for the God who comes to us so humbly, under the forms of bread and wine. We pray especially for [*add your intention*]. *Our Father – Hail Mary – Glory Be*

Fifth Day: You did not despise the learning of the pagans, and of those of other faiths, but drew it into the service of knowing and loving the one true God, the God of Abraham, Isaac, and Jacob; help us to see God's truth wherever it is to be found, and His hand at work in all He has made. We pray especially for [*add your intention*]. *Our Father – Hail Mary – Glory Be*

Sixth Day: You gave glory to God by your writing and thought; help us to place all the works of our hands and minds at the service of God and His Church. We pray especially for [*add your intention*]. *Our Father – Hail Mary – Glory Be*

Seventh Day: You delighted to teach, and to learn; teach us to know and love God as you did, and to recognize in all we experience the signs of his overwhelming love for us. We pray especially for [*add your intention*]. *Our Father – Hail Mary – Glory Be*

Eighth Day: You were above all a man of prayer; help us to discover that it is only in a relationship of prayer that we can come to know Him, who is the heart and goal of our Christian life. We pray especially for [*add your intention*]. *Our Father – Hail Mary – Glory Be*

Ninth Day: You knew that, however great our intellectual knowledge of God, it is like straw compared to the experience of his love. Help us not to let our own thoughts, concepts and plans become idols standing between us and the Father's overwhelming love for us. We pray especially for [*add your intention*]. *Our Father – Hail Mary – Glory Be*

Novena to St Josephine Bakhita

Feast Day: February 8th

Josephine Bakhita was born in Sudan in around 1869 but was abducted by slave traders at a young age and was so traumatized she forgot her own name. She is known by the cynical name given to her by her abductors – Bakhita, which means "Lucky". Bakhita was passed around from "owner" to "owner" and one of them had her body scarred with intricate patterns. Eventually she ended up with an Italian family who sent her to school with the Canossian sisters in Schio, Venice. There she was baptized Josephine. Contrary to the wishes of the family, she remained with the Canossians and became a religious. She was the doorkeeper of the order and was well loved by the local people for her deep compassion and sweetness which she didn't lose even during the long, painful illness which preceded her death. Josephine Bakhita was canonized in 2000.

First Day: St Josephine, you were taken from your family at an early age and lost your entire identity. We pray for all those children who have been abducted and for their parents and families who suffer not knowing what has become of them. Send your Holy Spirit to comfort them; and may they one day be reunited. We pray especially for [*add your intention*]. *Our Father – Hail Mary – Glory Be*

Second Day: You knew what it was to be a slave, to have no rights, to have lost even your name. We pray for the victims of people traffickers and all those in any kind of slavery. May this evil be wiped out from our world. We pray especially for [*add your intention*]. *Our Father – Hail Mary – Glory Be*

Third Day: St Josephine, one of your owners had your whole body scarred. You knew this terrible pain. We pray for all victims of torture. Help them to heal in body, mind and spirit. May all governments abandon this practice. We pray especially for [*add your intention*]. *Our Father – Hail Mary – Glory Be*

Fourth Day: Even in the terrible suffering of your life, you saw beauty in the world and believed there must be a God because of that beauty. May we too have something of your love for beauty and the natural world. We pray especially for [*add your intention*]. *Our Father – Hail Mary – Glory Be*

Fifth Day: When the family which had rescued you wanted you to leave the Canossians, you had the courage to refuse, even though you were truly grateful to them. Help us to put God's will above all things, even above our natural affections. We pray especially for [*add your intention*]. *Our Father – Hail Mary – Glory Be*

Sixth Day: St Josephine, you were so grateful to know God and to be part of his Church that you often kissed the baptismal font. May we never take for granted the faith we have been offered and give us something of your humility and gratitude for all God does. We pray especially for [*add your intention*]. *Our Father – Hail Mary – Glory Be*

Seventh Day: Your sufferings gave you great compassion for others and you were constantly smiling and always open to those who came to you, no matter how inconvenient it was. St Josephine, may we have something of your sweetness and openness, something of your joy. We pray especially for [*add your intention*]. *Our Father – Hail Mary – Glory Be*

Eighth Day: In your last painful illness you relived your slavery, begging the nurse to loosen your chains. We pray for all those who are weighed down by pain, and we ask that we too may enter the sufferings of our lives where God seems to have abandoned us. May we have the faith to know he has not. We pray especially for [*add your intention*]. *Our Father – Hail Mary – Glory Be*

Ninth Day: Your last words were "Our Lady, Our Lady". May we too know the comfort of the Mother of God, now and at the hour of our death. We pray especially for [*add your intention*]. *Our Father – Hail Mary – Glory Be*

Novena Prayer to St David

Feast Day: March 1st

We know almost nothing about the life of St David, who was a monk and bishop in south Wales in the late sixth century. He was widely venerated from the eighth century onwards, and his sanctity officially recognized by the Pope in 1120. There are many stories about his life, but it is not clear how many of them are historical. He is best-known as the patron saint of Wales. He is also patron of vegetarians and poets.

This prayer to St David can be said over nine days as a novena.

Prayer to St David

O God, who raised Blessed David to be an apostle and patron for your people in Wales, grant, we implore, that through his prayers the people may be restored to the truth which he taught, and to attain to everlasting life. Through Jesus Christ our Lord.

Amen

Novena to St John of God

Feast Day: March 8th

When John was eight years old he ran away from his home in Portugal and turned up in the Castile region of Spain where he worked as a shepherd. When he was old enough he became a mercenary and for the next eighteen years fought in various wars. He lost nearly all moral sense but when he was injured falling from his horse whilst out looting, he called on the Virgin Mary to save him and he was saved. This made an impression and when his company was disbanded when he was forty years old, he sought to put his life right with God. He wanted to be punished for his past life so pretended to be insane, since the "treatment" for that at the time was flogging. It was only when Blessed John of Avila intervened that he gave up the idea. He then started looking after the sick and set up several hospitals which he supported through work and begging. Others joined him and the Hospitaller Order began. He died aged fifty-five in 1550, his heart worn out in the service of the sick. He is patron of heart sufferers both because of his death through a weakened heart, and the great love he had for his neighbour. He was canonised in 1690 and declared patron of the dying and of hospitals in 1898.

First Day: You are the patron of all who suffer heart disease. We pray for them that they may find help for their illness. We also pray for all who are sick of heart whether through sin or unrequited longing. May they find and follow God's will. We pray especially for [*add your intention*]. *Our Father – Hail Mary – Glory Be*

Second Day: You ran away from home when you were young. We ask you to intercede for all runaways, that they may meet those who might help them, not those who might harm them. May we too not try to run away from the realities of our lives. We pray especially for [*add your intention*]. *Our Father – Hail Mary – Glory Be*

Third Day: You were a penitent sinner. We pray to know our sins and to repent of them and to know God's love and forgiveness. Awake in us a true love for the sacrament of penance and the courage to begin again. We pray especially for [*add your intention*]. *Our Father – Hail Mary – Glory Be*

Fourth Day: You listened to Blessed John of Avila when he told you to stop punishing yourself. May we also hear the voice of holy men and women in our lives and especially the voice of the Church, believing that is how God speaks to us. Grant us the humility to be able to obey. We pray especially for [*add your intention*]. *Our Father – Hail Mary – Glory Be*

Fifth Day: You worked tirelessly for the sick, spending your life in the service of others. We ask that you intercede for us that we may be healed of our spiritual sicknesses. We pray especially for [*add your intention*]. *Our Father – Hail Mary – Glory Be*

Sixth Day: You founded hospitals and worked to support them. We pray for all who work in hospitals, especially in areas where there is no funding. May they always trust in God and see him in their patients. We pray especially for [*add your intention*]. *Our Father – Hail Mary – Glory Be*

Seventh Day: You said, "Labour without ceasing to do all the good works you can while you still have the time". Grant us the grace to convert today. We pray especially for [*add your intention*]. *Our Father – Hail Mary – Glory Be*

Eighth Day: Before you worked for the sick, you sold religious books. We ask your blessing on all who make the Word known through the written word or other media. We pray especially for [*add your intention*]. *Our Father – Hail Mary – Glory Be*

Ninth Day: We pray for the dying, especially those who are dying alone. We ask you, their patron, to intercede for them before God. We pray especially for [*add your intention*]. *Our Father – Hail Mary – Glory Be*

Novena Prayer to St Patrick

Feast Day: March 17th

Although best known as patron saint of Ireland, St Patrick was in fact born in what is now England, son of a minor Roman official in (probably) the mid-fourth century. He was kidnapped by pirates as a boy, and taken as a slave to Ireland. He escaped after six years, but on his return to Britain discerned a call from God to bring Christ to the island of his captivity. The details of his later career are surrounded with many fabulous and legendary accretions, but we can be certain that he preached the Gospel widely in Ireland, was bishop to the Christian community there, and took a central role in the conversion of Ireland from paganism to Christianity. Devotion to him soon became very widespread, and from the eighth century onwards he was considered patron of Ireland.

This prayer to St Patrick can be said over nine days as a novena:

Prayer to St Patrick

God our Father, you sent Saint Patrick to preach your glory to the people of Ireland. By the help of his prayers, may all Christians proclaim your love to all men. Grant this through our Lord Jesus Christ, your Son, who lives and reigns with you and the Holy Spirit, one God, for ever and ever.

Amen

Novena to St Joseph

Feast Day: March 19th, May 1st (St Joseph the Worker)

 "Joseph, [Mary's] husband, ... was a righteous man" (Matthew 1.19).

St Joseph, husband of the Virgin Mary and foster-father of Jesus Christ, is one of the best-loved and most powerful intercessors. He is particularly invoked by husbands and fathers, by men in general, by those looking for work, by those with problems at work, and by those looking for somewhere to live. St Joseph is also known as the Protector of Holy Church, since he was entrusted by God with the care of the Virgin Mary (who is an image of the Church) and the child Jesus. He is also a strong guard against the assaults of the Enemy. Not least, he is the patron of a holy death, and so is often invoked by the dying.

First Day: As husband to Mary and foster-father to Jesus, you are an example of chastity, humility, faithfulness, and obedience to the word of God; intercede for us so that we too may be given these virtues in our lives, and may witness to God's power working in our weakness. We pray especially for [*add your intention*]. *Our Father – Hail Mary – Glory Be*

Second Day: You were chosen by God to be guardian and protector of Jesus and Mary; protect our homes and families; we ask your intercession for husbands and fathers, and for all those who bear responsibility for others. We pray especially for [*add your intention*]. *Our Father – Hail Mary – Glory Be*

Third Day: You know what it is like to have your own plans and expectations overturned by God's plans; help us to trust that He knows better than we do what we really need. We pray especially for [*add your intention*]. *Our Father – Hail Mary – Glory Be*

Fourth Day: You knew what it was like to be exiled from your homeland, to be without a stable place to live; we ask your intercession for those who are looking for somewhere to live, and for those who are far from home. We pray especially for [*add your intention*]. *Our Father – Hail Mary – Glory Be*

Fifth Day: When the child Jesus went missing, and was found in the Temple, you knew the pain of loss, and the joy of finding again; intercede for all who suffer the anguish of separation or bereavement, and help them to know that, like Jesus, we may all be found safe in our Father's house We pray especially for [*add your intention*]. *Our Father – Hail Mary – Glory Be*

Sixth Day: As you watched over Jesus and Mary on earth, now you are the Protector of the Universal Church; we ask your intercession for all who bear the name of Christian. We pray especially for [*add your intention*]. *Our Father – Hail Mary – Glory Be*

Seventh Day: In the silent witness of your life in Nazareth, the Church sees in you the model of our interior life with Christ; help us to pray, and to put our relationship with Jesus in prayer at the heart of our lives. We pray especially for [*add your intention*]. *Our Father – Hail Mary – Glory Be*

Eighth Day: You know what it is to work; help us to see the dignity and value of the tasks entrusted to us, and to believe that by humbly and faithfully doing what we have to do, we too may give glory to God whether the world recognises us or not. We pray especially for [*add your intention*]. *Our Father – Hail Mary – Glory Be*

Ninth Day: You are the model and patron of Christian death: we ask your intercession for all those who are close to death, and the grace of a holy death for them and for ourselves. We pray especially for [*add your intention*]. *Our Father – Hail Mary – Glory Be*

Novena to St Benedict

Feast Day: March 21st; July 11th (as Patron of Europe)

Benedict was a learned Roman of the fifth-sixth century who, inspired by the great monastic saints of Egypt, left public life to seek God in the wilderness (the closest equivalent to the Egyptian desert), living in community with others who felt a similar calling. They lived under a Rule which Benedict drew up, balancing work and prayer in solitude with a dedication to the great "work of God", the daily round of common prayer based on Scripture, especially the Psalms.

Like the saints of the desert, he was constantly aware of the attempts of the Devil to destroy his life with God, and was constant in his prayer to God against this peril. His powerful protection against the Enemy continues, and is often symbolized by the Benedictine Medal or Cross.

Benedict is regarded as the father of all monastic orders in the Western Church, and is one of the patrons of Europe. The monasteries that drew their life from his Rule played an essential, and providential, role in preserving and transmitting the learning and culture of the classical world, and in forming the religious life of Western Christendom. Most monks in the West today still live by a version of the Rule Benedict compiled almost a millenium and a half ago.

First Day: You were clear in your resolve to seek God alone, to be detached from anything that might impede this, and to persevere in these intentions. Help us to have the same determination to become the people – the saints – God sees us truly to be. We pray especially for [*add your intention*]. *Our Father – Hail Mary – Glory Be*

Second Day: You found God by being obedient to a rule of life, and in love for your brothers in Christ. Help us to keep our lives according to God's plan, and to love especially those we find most difficult. We pray especially for [*add your intention*]. *Our Father – Hail Mary – Glory Be*

Third Day: You were a father to the monks of your community, and remain the spiritual father of the whole Benedictine family. Help all Christian fathers – whether physical or spiritual – and all who exercise authority, to be icons of God's loving fatherhood. We pray especially for [*add your intention*]. *Our Father – Hail Mary – Glory Be*

Fourth Day: You drew up a Rule for the common life of your brothers to help them love God and their neighbour; help us to be lovingly obedient to those over us, firm yet kind to those in our charge, and thus to grow in love of God and of our brothers and sisters in Christ. We pray especially for [*add your intention*]. *Our Father – Hail Mary – Glory Be*

Fifth Day: Through you, God worked miracles of healing and deliverance; help us to recognize God's mighty deeds in our lives and in the world around us, and to be ourselves a sign to others of God's love and power, and to make this love present in God's world. We pray especially for [*add your intention*]. *Our Father – Hail Mary – Glory Be*

Sixth Day: You were granted even in this life a vision of God's glory, and were able to see both the insignificance of much that we worry about, and our supreme value in God's eyes. Help us to see with the eyes of faith, especially the loving care with which our Father treats us. We pray especially for [*add your intention*]. *Our Father – Hail Mary – Glory Be*

Seventh Day: You spread the Gospel by fearless preaching and your evident holiness of life. Help us to lead others to Christ by what we do as much as by what we say. We pray especially for [*add your intention*]. *Our Father – Hail Mary – Glory Be*

Eighth Day: You remain a strong protector against all the assaults and wiles of the Evil One. Strengthen us against his deceits and attacks, and help us not to believe the lying tales he spins around the facts of our lives, but to see in them only the hand of God, our loving Father. We pray especially for [*add your intention*]. *Our Father – Hail Mary – Glory Be*

Ninth Day: You held fast to God to the end, sustained by your faith in his promises, particularly by the promise of true happiness in the life that does not end or fail. Help us, too, to hear God's promises to us, and know that he will never cheat us, but desires only our true happiness. We pray especially for [*add your intention*]. *Our Father – Hail Mary – Glory Be*

Novena Prayer to St George

We all know St George as patron of England, and tamer of dragons. The facts of his life are obscure, but he seems to have been a Roman soldier, probably of the late third century, who was martyred at Lydda in Palestine during the great persecution by the Emperor Diocletian, probably for refusing to renounce Christ and worship the Emperor as a god. His cult was very widespread in the east from that time on; when English soldiers went to the Holy Land on Crusade, they were inspired by this warrior saint; Richard the Lionheart put himself and his army under St George's protection. From then on his popularity in England only grew: Edward III founded the Order of the Garter, with St George as patron, in 1348; Henry V called on St George for aid before the great victory of Agincourt in 1415. Thereafter he was secure as patron of England (although the patronage of two Anglo-Saxon Saint-Kings, Edward the Confessor and Edmund of East Anglia, was not neglected), and his popularity survived the spoliation and wreckage of the Reformation.

This prayer to St George can be said for nine days as a novena.

Prayer to St George

Faithful servant of God and invincible martyr, St George, inflamed with a burning love of Christ, you fought against the dragon of pride, falsehood, and deceit. Neither pain nor torture, nor the sword nor death could part you from the love of Christ.

I implore you for the sake of this love to help me by your intercession to overcome the temptations that surround me, and to bear bravely the trials that oppress me, so that I may patiently carry my cross, and let neither distress nor difficulty separate me from the love of our Lord, Jesus Christ.

Amen

Novena Prayer to St Peregrine

Feast day: May 1st

Peregrine Laziosi was born in 1265 in Forlì, a small town north east of Florence now probably most familiar as the destination of budget flights to "Bologna" (which is in fact forty miles away). In the late thirteenth century, however, Forlì was best known as a stronghold of opposition to the Papacy. In 1282, Pope Martin IV excommunicated the whole town. In an effort to resolve this situation, the Pope sent Fr (later Saint) Philip Benizi, who was head of the Servites, a newly founded order of friars who were much involved in caring for the sick, to preach to the townsfolk. Philip's visit was not a success: he was roughed up by a mob and thrown out of the town. One of those who assaulted him was the young Peregrine Laziosi.

This incident was a turning-point for Peregrine. He was gradually overcome with remorse for what he had done, and this led him to turn to God. He eventually joined the Servites, Philip's own order, as a lay-brother, when he was thirty years old.

He threw himself into their work of caring for the sick, especially during the frequent outbreaks of plague. Some time later, Peregrine himself fell ill, but not with the plague. He had a malignant growth on his leg that was so severe that the doctors proposed to amputate the whole limb. Peregrine spent a night in prayer before a crucifix, after which he was miraculously cured. As a result, he is considered a patron of cancer patients. Very many people can witness to the results of his intercession, whether physical healing, or the ability to accept their sufferings in peace. Peregrine died of old age in 1345; he was canonized in 1726.

This prayer to St Peregrine can be said over nine days as a novena.

Prayer to St Peregrine

God our Father, you are a God who loves me. I thank you for the many blessings you have given me. In loving trust I place myself before you. Let your healing love fill my life.

Give me the strength to understand my illness. Forgive my failures in carrying the cross. In St Peregrine you give us an example of patient suffering. Supported, then, by his prayers, I ask that the suffering I endure may be a source of life both now and for ever. I make this prayer through Christ, your Son.

Amen

Novena to the English Martyrs

Feast day: May 4th; (formerly October 25th)

The English Martyrs are those English Catholics who suffered death for the faith between the time of Henry VIII's breach with Rome in the early 1530's and the late seventeenth century. During this time, it was illegal even to attend Mass; priests celebrating the sacraments could be executed for treason. It was impossible to be educated as a Catholic, let alone train as a priest, in England; so thousands of English Catholics went abroad as exiles, to Italy, Spain, Portugal, and the Low Countries, so as eventually to return to England to keep the faith alive.

The exact number of martyrs for the faith in England during these years is known only to God. Of those of whom we have record, over forty have been canonized, and several hundred beatified. There are some hundreds more whose causes are still open, or have been postponed owing to incomplete evidence.

They were a very disparate group of people – many were priests executed for saying Mass, others laity who helped them, or simply refused to deny their faith under persecution. They came from all classes of society, rich and poor, educated and unlettered; but they were alike in placing their faith above any material advantage, and indeed valuing it more than life itself. Their witness to Christ is one of the glories of the Church in England, and their intercession for us now one of its greatest treasures.

First Day: You endured exile from your country and your families for love of God and the faith. Help all who live in exile today; and help us to value our faith above our securities. We pray especially for [*add your intention*]. *Our Father - Hail Mary - Glory Be*

Second Day: You had the courage to witness for Christ before men without counting the cost. Help us to have this same courage in our day. We pray especially for [*add your intention*]. *Our Father - Hail Mary - Glory Be*

Third Day: You loved England, your country, enough to suffer exile, persecution, and death to proclaim Jesus Christ here. Intercede for England, and for all who are called to proclaim Christ here today. We pray especially for [*add your intention*]. *Our Father - Hail Mary - Glory Be*

Fourth Day: You had a great love of the sacraments, especially the Eucharist, for which you were ready to give up your lives. Help us to have something of this same love, and never to take for granted these great gifts of God. We pray especially for [*add your intention*]. *Our Father - Hail Mary - Glory Be*

Fifth Day: You had a profound love of truth, and would not deny it even though this meant suffering and death. Give us the same love of truth, and zeal for the faith, that you had.

We pray especially for [*add your intention*]. *Our Father - Hail Mary - Glory Be*

Sixth Day: At the heart of all you did and endured was the love of God. Help us to know this love, and to pass it to our neighbour. We pray especially for [*add your intention*]. *Our Father - Hail Mary - Glory Be*

Seventh Day: You had such compassion for sinners that you risked all that they might be converted and live. Help us not to judge others, but to show God's merciful love to all; help us, too, not to despair of our own sins, but to lay them humbly before the Father who loves us. We pray especially for [*add your intention*]. *Our Father - Hail Mary - Glory Be*

Eighth Day: You readily forgave those who persecuted you, and offered your sufferings for their conversion. Intercede for us to have something of the same spirit in the face of injustice or persecution. We pray especially for [*add your intention*]. *Our Father - Hail Mary - Glory Be*

Ninth Day: You persevered in your witness to the end, and joyfully accepted the sufferings that opened to you the Kingdom. Intercede for us, and for those who are near to death, or undergoing a trial of faith, that we too may have the grace of final perseverance. We pray especially for [*add your intention*]. *Our Father - Hail Mary - Glory Be*

Novena to St Damien of Molokai

Feast day: May 10th

Damien de Veuster was born in Belgium in 1840 into a Flemish-speaking family of grain merchants. His parents wanted him to go into the family business but when he wanted to join the Congregation of the Sacred Hearts of Jesus and Mary, like his older brother, they did not stand in his way. Damien's older brother was meant to go to Hawaii to the missions, but when he became ill Damien arranged to take his place. Once ordained and given his own parish, Damien was full of energy – evangelizing, building churches, farming, ministering to his parishioners, and debunking voodoo. Later he volunteered to be the resident priest on Molokai, a horrific leper colony, where he set about the physical and spiritual care of the sufferers, changing their lives until he himself died of the disease sixteen years later. He was only forty-nine. He was beatified in 1995 and canonized in 2009. He is considered patron of those with leprosy, those suffering from HIV/AIDS, and all those cast out by society. He is also patron of the American state of Hawaii.

First Day: You were sent away to school in a region where you didn't speak the language and people tried to bully you because of it. We pray for those who are bullied whether at school or at work or in whatever situation. May they emulate you in not accepting it. We pray especially for [*add your intention*]. *Our Father - Hail Mary - Glory Be*

Second Day: You loved your parents but you loved God more. You knew God was calling you to the priesthood and you answered that call although you knew your parents had other hopes of you. May we put God first and never refuse his call because of any other attachment. We pray especially for [*add your intention*]. *Our Father - Hail Mary - Glory Be*

Third Day: You gave up family, country and language to go and evangelize, knowing that you would never see your home or family again. Accord us something of your courage and clear-sightedness. We pray especially for [*add your intention*]. *Our Father - Hail Mary - Glory Be*

Fourth Day: In Hawaii you worked tirelessly, giving everything to make Christ known. We pray that we can value our faith as much as you did. We pray especially for [*add your intention*]. *Our Father - Hail Mary - Glory Be*

Fifth Day: When you went to Molokai you were prepared to give up your life to serve others. Help us to understand this Christian love and to begin to desire it for ourselves. We pray especially for [*add your intention*]. *Our Father - Hail Mary - Glory Be*

Sixth Day: When you first arrived in the leper colony you were revolted by the patients, but you didn't let them see this and continued to work for them. We pray to have this spirit so we can put others first, thinking of their needs and feelings rather than our own. We pray especially for [*add your intention*]. *Our Father - Hail Mary - Glory Be*

Seventh Day: You didn't deal well with bureaucracy and often offended people by your brusqueness. You had to learn to ask forgiveness. May we never think God cannot use us because of our character, and may we too have the humility to ask pardon of those we have offended. We pray especially for [*add your intention*]. *Our Father - Hail Mary - Glory Be*

Eighth Day: You suffered greatly on Molokai because you were cut off from the sacraments, especially the sacrament of reconciliation. May we understand the importance of this sacrament and have recourse to it often. We pray especially for [*add your intention*]. *Our Father - Hail Mary - Glory Be*

Ninth Day: You suffered terrible loneliness and turned to the Blessed Sacrament for comfort. We pray for all who are lonely. Help us to give time to anyone we know who is lonely, and to give time to Christ in the Blessed Sacrament. We pray especially for [*add your intention*]. *Our Father - Hail Mary - Glory Be*

Novena to St Dymphna

Feast day: May 15th

Tradition says St Dymphna was a seventh century Irish princess, daughter of a Christian mother and a pagan father. Tragically, her mother died when Dymphna was a young teenager and Dymphna's father, the balance of his mind disturbed, tried to marry his own daughter. Dymphna went for help to a priest, Father Gerebran who, understanding that the king, her father, had the power to do whatever he wanted, advised her to flee the country. Fr Gerebran and two others escaped with Dymphna to Gheel in modern-day Belgium. Her father tracked her down however, and when she refused to return with him killed Fr Gerebran and Dymphna, cutting off their heads with his sword. They were buried in tombs by the local people and soon there were reports of the miraculous healing at Dymphna's tomb of the mentally ill and those suffering from epilepsy. More and more mentally ill people came to the shrine and the local people began to look after them in their homes, a tradition which continues today. St Dymphna is patron of those suffering mental illness or epilepsy, and also patron of family harmony.

First Day: St Dymphna, one of your parents was Christian but the other was not and you lived with two different views of the world. We pray for all families which are divided by religion. Intercede for them and bring harmony; help them to live together in love and respect. We pray especially for [*add your intention*]. *Our Father - Hail Mary - Glory Be*

Second Day: You lost your mother when you were a young teenager. We pray for all children who have lost one or both parents through death, divorce or other separation. We ask you to comfort them and help them to experience God's love for them. We pray especially for [*add your intention*]. *Our Father - Hail Mary - Glory Be*

Third Day: Your father was destroyed by grief. We pray for all those who grieve, especially those who do not know the hope of eternal life or those whose grief is affecting their sanity. Intercede for them that they can receive hope and comfort. We pray especially for [*add your intention*]. *Our Father - Hail Mary - Glory Be*

Fourth Day: You had to flee your homeland. We pray for all refugees and those escaping from danger, especially danger in their own families. Intercede that they may find people to help and succour them. We pray especially for [*add your intention*]. *Our Father - Hail Mary - Glory Be*

Fifth Day: You had to run away from home to avoid incest. We pray for all those who have been sexually abused, especially those who have been abused in their own families. We pray for the healing of their self-worth. We pray especially for [*add your intention*]. *Our Father - Hail Mary - Glory Be*

Sixth Day: You are the patron of those with mental illness. We pray for all those who suffer from mental illness and for their families. We pray that they do not lose hope or sight of God. We pray especially for [*add your intention*]. *Our Father - Hail Mary - Glory Be*

Seventh Day: As the sick came to your shrine to be cured, people began to care for and look after them. We pray for all those who work with the mentally ill. We pray that they see in their charges the face of Christ, and always guard their dignity. We pray especially for [*add your intention*]. *Our Father - Hail Mary - Glory Be*

Eighth Day: You lost your mother to death but your father to mental illness and abuse. We pray for all those who have lost their parents to mental illness or addiction, and for all whose parents have treated them badly. Intercede for them that they may be able to forgive. We pray especially for [*add your intention*]. *Our Father - Hail Mary - Glory Be*

Ninth Day: We ask you to intercede for us all, that we might be cured of our delusions and misconceptions whether about ourselves or others. We pray for a healing of our family history. We pray especially for [*add your intention*]. *Our Father - Hail Mary - Glory Be*

Novena to St Rita

Feast day: May 22nd

 Rita Lotti was born to elderly parents near Cascia, in the Italian region of Umbria, around 1381. She wanted to join the convent and become a nun, but instead obeyed her parents and got married. Her marriage was a difficult one and her husband was eventually killed in a vendetta. When her sons planned to avenge their father, Rita prayed that they wouldn't commit murder, even if it meant they die first. Both of them died from illness soon afterwards. Rita then tried to enter the convent, but the community was reluctant to take her. She did not give up, and waited for God to make it possible. In the meantime, she brokered peace between her husband's family and that of his murderer, thus ending the vendetta. Finally she was accepted into the convent.

One day, when she was praying for a share in Christ's sufferings, a thorn from Christ's crown of thorns pierced her forehead. She suffered the pain of the resulting suppurating wound for the rest of her life. She is known to be effective in making peace, especially in families, and is called the saint of things despaired of.

First Day: You wanted to enter the convent but your parents arranged a marriage for you. We pray for those whose hopes have been frustrated. We pray especially for [*add your intention*]. *Our Father - Hail Mary - Glory Be*

Second Day: You lived for many years with a difficult husband at a time when there was no escape. You never stopped praying for him. We pray for all those fleeing from or experiencing domestic violence. We pray especially for [*add your intention*]. *Our Father - Hail Mary - Glory Be*

Third Day: You wanted the best for your sons even if it meant their death. Help all mothers of difficult children to pray for them, and to entrust them to God's providence and mercy. We pray especially for [*add your intention*]. *Our Father - Hail Mary - Glory Be*

Fourth Day: You brokered peace between your husband's family and the family of his murderer. We ask you to intercede anywhere in our lives there is discord and hatred. We pray especially for [*add your intention*]. *Our Father - Hail Mary - Glory Be*

Fifth Day: You did everything God asked of you, but he didn't give you your heart's desire. Help us not to become bitter if God has not rewarded us as we think we deserve. May we humbly ask his will. We pray especially for [*add your intention*]. *Our Father - Hail Mary - Glory Be*

Sixth Day: You persevered in your desire to enter the convent, waiting on God's time. Eventually everything became easy and you were able to enter. Help us to persevere in prayer for our intentions and trustingly accept God's will whatever the outcome. We pray especially for [*add your intention*]. *Our Father - Hail Mary - Glory Be*

Seventh Day: You endured painful illness and the rejection of your sisters because of the terrible stench of your wound. You accepted this in peace. May we too learn to accept suffering and rejection, knowing God will never reject us. We pray especially for [*add your intention*]. *Our Father - Hail Mary - Glory Be*

Eighth Day: You were famed for your compassion and wisdom and many people came to ask your help. Intercede for us that we can be open to others. We pray especially for [*add your intention*]. *Our Father - Hail Mary - Glory Be*

Ninth Day: You are the saint of things despaired of. We pray that you intercede for us in this thing which seems impossible. We pray especially for [*add your intention*]. *Our Father - Hail Mary - Glory Be*

Novena to St Anthony of Padua

Feast day: June 13th

 St Anthony of Padua was actually born in Portugal, towards the end of the twelfth century. He joined the new order of friars that had recently been founded by St Francis, and moved to Italy. He was a very famous preacher, and was known for his great love for the poor – many churches still collect money for "St Anthony's Bread", for the poor and hungry. He is usually shown with a book, on which the child Jesus is seated. This shows his strong love for Christ as he is present in the proclaimed Word of the Scriptures.

He is very well-known as an intercessor for those who need to find something that has been lost. This apparently stems from a time when one of the friars borrowed his prayer-book without asking, and Anthony appeared to him in a fearsome vision. Whatever the origin of this, St Anthony is undeniably effective in finding lost items – whether physical objects (anything from car keys upwards) or spiritual things, including faith, hope, and love.

The best-known novena to St Anthony is known as the Nine Tuesdays, because it is usually said (as the name suggests) on nine successive Tuesdays; however you could certainly make it on nine consecutive days instead. We give a version of it here.

First Day: Blessed St Anthony, I greet you in the name of the Virgin Mary, Queen of the Angels. I ask you, with her, to bring my request before Almighty God. We pray especially for [*add your intention*]. *Our Father - Hail Mary - Glory Be*

41

Second Day: Blessed St Anthony, I greet you in the name of the patriarchs and prophets. Like them, you were given the gift of knowledge, even knowledge of the future. I ask you, with them, to bring my request before Almighty God. We pray especially for [*add your intention*]. *Our Father - Hail Mary - Glory Be*

Third Day: Blessed St Anthony, I greet you in the name of all Christ's holy apostles and disciples. God chose you, too, to preach the Gospel and spread the faith. I ask you, with them, to bring my request before Almighty God. We pray especially for [*add your intention*]. *Our Father - Hail Mary - Glory Be*

Fourth Day: Blessed St Anthony, like the martyrs and saints who proclaimed Christ, you were always ready to suffer persecution for his sake I ask you, with them, to bring my request before Almighty God. We pray especially for [*add your intention*]. *Our Father - Hail Mary - Glory Be*

Fifth Day: Blessed St Anthony, I greet you in the name of all holy bishops and priests. Like them, you were given the grace to convert many to Christ. I ask you, with them, to bring my request before Almighty God. We pray especially for [*add your intention*]. *Our Father - Hail Mary - Glory Be*

Sixth Day: Blessed St Anthony, I greet you and bless God for you, because he gave you the grace to spend your life in good works, like so many holy monks and hermits. You too kept vigil, prayed, fasted, and denied yourself. May your prayers and theirs rise before God on my behalf. We pray especially for [*add your intention*]. *Our Father - Hail Mary - Glory Be*

Seventh Day: Blessed St Anthony, I greet you in the name of all holy virgins and innocents. Like them, you led a life of purity and overcame temptations against it. I ask you, together with them, to pray to God for me. We pray especially for [*add your intention*]. *Our Father - Hail Mary - Glory Be*

Eighth Day: Blessed St Anthony, I greet you in the name of all holy widows, and all holy husbands and wives, and I bless God for all of your virtues. You, like these holy men and women, served God faithfully here on earth; I ask you and them to pray for me now. We pray especially for [*add your intention*]. *Our Father - Hail Mary - Glory Be*

Ninth Day: Blessed St Anthony, I greet you in the name of St Joseph, most chaste husband of the Blessed Virgin Mary. I greet you in the name of all holy men and women now living. I bless the most high God for giving you so much of his love and grace. I ask you, and them, to speak to God for me; may my request be granted if it is for God's greater glory, and for my salvation. We pray especially for [*add your intention*]. *Our Father - Hail Mary - Glory Be*

Novena to St Thomas More

Feast day: June 22nd

Thomas More was born in London in 1478. He married and had four children and after the death of his first wife married again. More was a devoted father who made sure his daughters were educated as well as his son - unusual in those days. He was also very successful in his career, being a lawyer, then a judge known for his fairness and incorruptibility and finally becoming Lord Chancellor. As well as this he was a theologian, author and personal friend of the king. But when he had to choose between all of this and faith, he chose faith, entering into the consequences of that with his eyes wide open. He could not in conscience say that Henry VIII's marriage to Catherine of Aragon was not valid, or that the King was head of the Church in England, and he was imprisoned and executed for treason because of this. He was canonized in 1935 and shares a feast day with St John Fisher, a bishop martyred for the same reasons. He is often seen as patron of politicians and all those in public life, and of all trying to live Christian lives in the world.

First Day: You were a devoted family man, lovingly involved in the lives of your children, providing security for them and making sure they were well equipped for life. We pray for all fathers that they may give time to their children and show interest in their lives. We pray especially for [*add your intention*]. *Our Father - Hail Mary - Glory Be*

Second Day: You were successful in your career, but were also known for your integrity. Intercede for us that we may be honest and hard-working in our professions.We pray especially for [*add your intention*]. *Our Father - Hail Mary - Glory Be*

Third Day: As a lawyer, judge and statesman you were known for your fairness and incorruptibility. We pray for all those in the law and in politics, that they may be motivated not by greed or personal gain but by honesty and altruism.

Fourth Day: You were well known for your sense of humour and love of life. You were even able to make jokes on the scaffold. Intercede for us that we may learn truly to enjoy life and to learn how to be happy in all situations. We pray especially for [*add your intention*]. *Our Father - Hail Mary - Glory Be*

Fifth Day: You knew your faith and learned how to defend it. Help us to learn to do the same, so that we can have a solid foundation on which to base our lives and a way of passing the Gospel to others. We pray especially for [*add your intention*]. *Our Father - Hail Mary - Glory Be*

Sixth Day: You were not afraid to be the lone voice of truth even when you knew it could cost you everything. Intercede for us that we may be able to stand up for the teachings of the Church even when they are unpopular. We pray especially for [*add your intention*]. *Our Father - Hail Mary - Glory Be*

Seventh Day: You were finally betrayed by someone you had helped. May we too learn to forgive those who have betrayed our trust. We pray especially for [*add your intention*]. *Our Father - Hail Mary - Glory Be*

Eighth Day: You submitted to God's will and had faith that even if you betrayed him in your anguish, he would pull you up again as he did St Peter. Help us to learn the humility of accepting failure, and to trust in God's will. We pray especially for [*add your intention*]. *Our Father - Hail Mary - Glory Be*

Ninth Day: You went to your death in the sure hope of eternal life. Give us too something of your faith, your hope and your courage. We pray especially for [*add your intention*]. *Our Father - Hail Mary - Glory Be*

Novena Prayer to St John Fisher

Feast day: June 22nd

 Like St Thomas More, St John Fisher was martyred for refusing to put his conscience, and his love for truth and the Church of Christ, second to the demands of the secular power, in the person of King Henry VIII. Fisher was the only one of the English Bishops who was brave enough to do this; the others were intimidated into submission, or were willing to compromise in the fond belief that the matter of the King's divorce, and the governance of the Church, was ultimately secondary or unimportant.

John Fisher was a Yorkshireman, born in 1469, and had a successful academic career (he was central to the renewal in England of scholarship in the ancient languages of Greek and Hebrew) before he was made Bishop of Rochester, England's smallest and poorest see, in 1504. He refused to move to a richer or more important diocese, and was diligent in his pastoral duties. He was also a world-famous theologian, and confessor to the Queen, Catherine of Aragon, whom Henry VIII wanted to repudiate. Henry went to great lengths to persuade Fisher to support him, but the saint refused to put his own advantage before the truth, that the marriage was valid and no amount of the King's bullying could make it otherwise. He was imprisoned on a trumped-up charge, and then executed on June 22nd 1535, not before the then Pope had made him a Cardinal. Four hundred years later, another Pope declared him a saint.

This prayer, composed by St John Fisher himself, can suitably be said over nine days as a novena

Prayer to St John Fisher

I know, most gracious Father, that thou art here present with me albeit I see thee not. But thou both seest me and hearest me and no secrecy of my heart is hid from thee. Thou hearest that I now ask thine Holy Spirit and thou knowest that I now pray therefore and that I am very desirous to have the same. Lo! Dear Father, with all the enforcement of my heart I beseech thee to give thine Holy Spirit unto me. Wherefore unless thou wilt disappoint the promise of thy son Jesu thou canst not but give me this Holy Spirit; so by this means I shall be fully relieved of that misery whereof I complained unto thy goodness at the beginning. Thy most Holy Spirit he shall make me to love thee with all my heart, and with all my soul, with all my mind, with all my power, for he is the author of all good love, he is the very furnace of charity and he is the fountain of all gracious affections and godly desires.

Amen

Novena Prayer to St Christopher

Feast day: July 25th

St Christopher (whose name means "the one who bears Christ") seems to have been martyred for being a Christian some time before the mid-fifth century, probably in the third century, in the Roman province of Bithynia (where we know there were Christian communites at the start of the second century) in Asia Minor. He is best known because of a story in a medieval version of his life, which says that he was a giant who had been a pagan, but after becoming a Christian served the community by carrying travellers on his back across a wide river. One day he carried a small child who, despite his size, was so heavy Christopher barely made it safely across. The child was Christ, and the weight was that of the whole world and its creator. Whatever we may think of this as history, it is a powerful reminder that Christian service to others is also service to Christ. St Christopher is very well-known as patron of travellers in general, of all who have journeys to make, and of motorists especially.

Prayer to St Christopher

St Christopher, you gained a beautiful name, Christbearer, from the wonderful legend that while carrying people across a raging stream, you also carried the Child Jesus. Teach us to be true Christbearers to those who do not know Him. Protect drivers, and all who transport those who bear Christ within them. Keep safe all who travel, especially [*make your request*], and bring us all safe to our final journey's end, in God.

Amen

Novena to St Anne

Anne is the name tradition gives to the mother of the Blessed Virgin Mary. It is said that she and her husband Joachim were a good and holy couple who were unable to have children for many years and suffered humiliation because of this. Finally the Virgin Mary was born to them and they brought her up to love God, and found a man of faith, St Joseph, for her to marry.

Again as tradition has it, she had much to do with the bringing up of Jesus himself, and after the death of Joachim she followed the Holy Family to Egypt. Tradition says also that when Martha, Mary and Lazarus went to France after Christ's death and resurrection, they took with them the bones of St Anne.

A legend says St Anne was married three times, and this is why many people pray for her intercession to find a good husband. This is the origin of the humorous prayer, "Holy St Anne, Holy St Anne, find me a man, as fast as you can". Whether or not this legend is true, St Anne is known to help in these cases, finding good husbands for women, as she did for her own daughter.

First Day: You and your husband truly loved God but it seemed your piety went unrewarded. We pray to persevere, and not to lose hope in God's love. We pray especially for [*add your intention*]. *Our Father - Hail Mary - Glory Be*

Second Day: You had to see your husband's humiliation without being able to do anything. Help us not to be shocked or scandalized by the sufferings of our loved ones, and to believe God also loves them. We pray especially for [*add your intention*]. *Our Father - Hail Mary - Glory Be*

Third Day: When you finally had a child, you did not make her an idol but brought her up to love God. Help all Christian parents to bring up their children in the faith. We pray especially for [*add your intention*]. *Our Father - Hail Mary - Glory Be*

Fourth Day: When your daughter was pregnant before being married, it seemed she had betrayed everything you taught her. Help us when we are disappointed in people not to judge too quickly. We pray especially for [*add your intention*]. *Our Father - Hail Mary - Glory Be*

Fifth Day: You were a loving grandmother. We pray for all grandparents, that they may bring love and wisdom to their grandchildren's lives. We pray especially for [*add your intention*]. *Our Father - Hail Mary - Glory Be*

Sixth Day: You followed the Holy Family into exile in Egypt. We pray for all older people who are uprooted later in life, and for all older people whose families live far away. We pray especially for [*add your intention*]. *Our Father - Hail Mary - Glory Be*

Seventh Day: You were so inspiring that Martha, Mary and Lazarus took your bones with them on their missionary journey. Help us to see that older people still have much to offer us. We pray especially for [*add your intention*]. *Our Father - Hail Mary - Glory Be*

Eighth Day: You are known to help those looking for husbands. We ask you to intercede for all those looking for Christian husbands or wives. We pray especially for [*add your intention*]. *Our Father - Hail Mary - Glory Be*

Ninth Day: You are also patroness of women in labour. We pray for all women giving birth, for all children born today, and for all those who have been aborted. We pray especially for [*add your intention*]. *Our Father - Hail Mary - Glory Be*

Novena to St Martha

Feast day: July 29th

 St Martha lived with her brother Lazarus and sister Mary in Bethany. Jesus often visited them there. Martha was the one who looked after the house, and is therefore the patron of cooks and homemakers. The Gospels record an incident where Martha complained to Jesus that he had not told her sister Mary to help her with serving their guests, but let her sit and listen to him. Jesus told Martha not to worry about so many things; and that her sister was right to put listening to him first.

Martha later recognized Jesus as the Messiah, and witnessed him raise her brother Lazarus from the dead. After the Resurrection of Jesus, it is said that she and her brother and sister evangelized in France, where Martha converted many people through her preaching, calling them away from the worship of a dragon god.

First Day: Yours was a home that Christ himself was comfortable in. We ask you help us to be hospitable and open and to make our homes a place where Christ can be present. We pray especially for [*add your intention*]. *Our Father - Hail Mary - Glory Be*

Second Day: You worked hard in your house. Help us to give value to housework and the routine tasks of life. Intercede for us so that we can look after others' needs with serenity and joy. We pray especially for [*add your intention*]. *Our Father - Hail Mary - Glory Be*

Third Day: You served Christ. Help us to serve him in our own lives. We pray especially for [*add your intention*]. *Our Father - Hail Mary - Glory Be*

Fourth Day: Help us to work for the good of others, but always to put Christ first. Help us also to learn from Christ, as you did, not to worry and fret, but to trust in God's all-powerful providence. We pray especially for [*add your intention*]. *Our Father - Hail Mary - Glory Be*

Fifth Day: The Lord rebuked you for your judgement, anger and self importance and you accepted it. You knew he loved you. We ask that we may be able to accept criticism without remaining resentful and without being destroyed by it. We pray especially for [*add your intention*]. *Our Father - Hail Mary - Glory Be*

Sixth Day: You recognised Jesus as the Christ when he came to your house after your brother's death. Help us to recognise Christ in our lives and to know his love and power. We pray especially for [*add your intention*]. *Our Father - Hail Mary - Glory Be*

Seventh Day: You saw Christ raise your brother from the dead. Intercede for us so our eyes can be opened to the miracles Christ has done in our lives. We pray especially for [*add your intention*]. *Our Father - Hail Mary - Glory Be*

Eighth Day: Christ changed your life. Tradition says that you evangelized in France with your brother and sister. Help us not to be disappointed with our lives but to believe that life can be much more than we ever imagined, in ways we never thought possible. We pray especially for [*add your intention*]. *Our Father - Hail Mary - Glory Be*

Ninth Day: Tradition says you tamed a dragon, turning people away from worshipping a dragon god by your inspired preaching. Help us to see how God can do great things with small people if only we are open to his will. We pray especially for [*add your intention*]. *Our Father - Hail Mary - Glory Be*

Novena Prayer to St Teresa Benedicta of the Cross (Edith Stein)

Feast day: August 9th

Edith Stein was born into a prosperous Jewish family in what is now Poland. She was a well-known philosopher and teacher who converted to Catholicism, became a Carmelite nun, and was murdered in Auschwitz, a martyr for the Jewish people.

Prayer to St Teresa Benedicta of the Cross

God of our fathers, at the hour of her martyrdom you brought St Teresa Benedicta to the fullness of the knowledge of the cross. Fill us with that same knowledge and may we, through the intercession of St Teresa Benedicta, always seek you the Supreme Truth and remain faithful to the covenant of love ratified in the blood of your Son.

Amen

Novena to St Maximilian Kolbe

Feast day: August 14th

 Maximilian Kolbe was born in 1894 of a Polish mother and ethnic German father. In 1914 his father was hanged by the Russian army after fighting for an independent Poland. As a child, Maximilian had a vision of the Blessed Virgin who offered him the crown of purity or the crown of martyrdom. He chose both. He initially thought of joining the army but instead became a Franciscan priest. He founded a "village" of religious dedicated to Mary Immaculate and a small religious newspaper which became hugely influential in Poland. In 1930 he and four companions went to Japan where they worked for six years. Maximilian suffered poor health all the time he was there but did not think of giving up. Soon after his return to Poland, the country was invaded by the Nazis and he was arrested, and was eventually sent to Auschwitz. He ministered to his fellow prisoners before finally offering his life in exchange for that of a married man who was one of ten prisoners sentenced to be locked up and left to starve to death. Fr Maximilian encouraged the other prisoners in his death cell, and announced the Gospel even as they all starved to death. Finally only he was left alive and was murdered by lethal injection, accepting death with peace.

First Day: When still a child you entrusted your future to the Mother of God and accepted the crowns of purity and martyrdom. Help us to learn to be generous with our lives in the service of God. We pray especially for [*add your intention*]. *Our Father - Hail Mary - Glory Be*

Second Day: You had a great love of the military and thought of joining the army but instead began the Militia Immaculata to work for the conversion of sinners. We remember all those who serve in the armed forces and their families. We pray especially for [*add your intention*]. *Our Father - Hail Mary - Glory Be*

Third Day: You began a small religious newspaper which led to an upsurge of faith amongst your countrymen. May we too realise that nothing we do is too small for God to use.
We pray especially for [*add your intention*]. *Our Father - Hail Mary - Glory Be*

Fourth Day: You had such zeal for the proclamation of the Gospel that you went to Japan with no money and no word of the language and what you built is now the centre of the Franciscan province there. May we share in your zeal to announce the Good News through our words and our lives.
We pray especially for [*add your intention*]. *Our Father - Hail Mary - Glory Be*

Fifth Day: When the Nazis had invaded your country and you were under suspicion you said, "No one in the world can change truth". May we hold firm to the one who is the Truth, Jesus Christ. We pray especially for [*add your intention*]. *Our Father - Hail Mary - Glory Be*

Sixth Day: In prison you were asked whether you believed in Christ and were beaten every time you said you did. You persevered in your witness. May we still hold fast to Christ even in suffering or pain, and if we are persecuted for that belief may we have the courage not to desert him. We pray especially for [*add your intention*]. *Our Father - Hail Mary - Glory Be*

Seventh Day: Even when you were sent to Auschwitz you did not abandon your vocation as priest. Although you were beaten almost to death you still heard confessions and spoke of Christ's love. We ask you to give us something of your conviction and courage in front of the sufferings of our lives. We pray especially for [*add your intention*]. *Our Father - Hail Mary - Glory Be*

Eighth Day: When a fellow prisoner was sentenced to death by starvation you volunteered to take his place: to die so that he had a chance of life. May we always remember the words of Our Lord, "he who loses his life for my sake will find it" and give us the courage to lose our lives in whatever way is asked of us. We pray especially for [*add your intention*]. *Our Father - Hail Mary - Glory Be*

Ninth Day: Because you were killed by an injection of carbolic acid, you are the patron of drug users. We pray for all those who suffer this terrible addiction and for their families. May they have the courage and help they need to turn their lives around. We pray especially for [*add your intention*]. *Our Father - Hail Mary - Glory Be*

Novena Prayer to St Helena

Feast day: August 18th

St Helena was Empress of Rome, and mother of the Emperor Constantine, who in 313 gave the Christian faith official standing within the Roman Empire. Legend makes Helena a British princess, perhaps daughter to Coel, King of the Trinovantes ("Old King Cole" of the nursery rhyme); certainly, she became a Christian before her son did. In her old age, she made a tour of the Holy Land, visiting the places associated with Christ's life, death, and resurrection. During this visit, she found the relics of the True Cross, long hidden in Jerusalem, relics much of which have survived and are venerated even to this day. St Helena witnesses to the historical reality of Jesus, the Incarnate God, in an age when many were confused by theological speculation and fashionable "gnostic" religions, similar to the "new age" notions of today. She also shows us that holiness is not confined to those who are literally poor or obscure, but can be found by anyone, whatever their state in life, who is ready to do God's will as it is given to them. She is also patron of archaeologists. Her tomb is in the church of St Maria in Aracoeli on the Capitoline hill in Rome. There is a superb life of St Helena, in a fictionalized form, by the English Catholic writer Evelyn Waugh.

A traditional prayer to St Helena

Holy St Helena, with the anguish and devotion with which you sought the Cross of Christ, I plead that you give me God's grace to suffer patiently the labours of this life so that through them and with your intercession and protection I may seek and carry the cross that God has given me, so that I can serve him in this life and be with him in the next.

Amen

From Evelyn Waugh's "Helena", a prayer made by the Empress to the Three Wise Men before finding the Cross (this could also be used as a novena prayer before the Epiphany, January 6th):

Like me, you were late in coming. The shepherds were here long before; even the cattle. They had joined the chorus of angels before you were on your way. For you the primordial discipline of the heavens was relaxed and a new defiant light blazed amid the disconcerted stars.

How laboriously you came, taking sights and calculating, where the shepherds had run barefoot! How odd you looked on the road, attended by what outlandish liveries, laden with such preposterous gifts!

You came at length to the final stage of your pilgrimage and the great star stood still above you. What did you do? You stopped to call on King Herod. Deadly exchange of compliments in which began that unended war of mobs and magistrates against the innocent!

Yet you came, and were not turned away. You too found room before the manger. Your gifts were not needed, but they were accepted and put carefully away, for they were brought with love. In that new order of charity that had just come to life, there was room for you, too. You were not lower in the eyes of the holy family than the ox or the ass.

You are my especial patrons, and patrons of all latecomers, of all who have a tedious journey to make to the truth, of all who are confused with knowledge and speculation, of all who through politeness make themselves partners in guilt, of all who stand in danger by reason of their talents.

For His sake who did not reject your curious gifts, pray always for the learned, the oblique, the delicate. Let them not be quite forgotten at the Throne of God when the simple come into their kingdom.

Novena Prayer to St Monica

Feast day: August 27th

Monica was the Christian wife of a difficult husband and mother of two sons, one of whom lived a dissolute life and then joined a cult. She never stopped praying for him and eventually he converted and became the great St Augustine of Hippo. She is the especial patron of those who have difficult marriages or wayward children.

Prayer to St Monica

Holy St Monica, troubled wife and mother, many sorrows pierced your heart during your lifetime but you never despaired or lost faith. With confidence and persistence you prayed for the conversion of your husband, and of your son, Augustine. Your prayers were answered. Grant me that same patience, fortitude and trust in the Lord. Intercede for me before the Lord [*make your request*] and grant that I may have the grace to accept his will in all things.

Amen

Novena to St Pio of Pietrelcina (Padre Pio)

Feast day: September 23rd

Francesco Forgione, universally known as Padre Pio (his name in religious life), was born to a peasant family in southern Italy in 1887. He became a Capuchin friar in 1903. His intense prayer life, and identification with the sufferings of Christ, took physical expression in the stigmata, or signs of the wounds of Christ's passion (in hands, feet, and side) that appeared on his body soon after he was ordained priest in 1910. He prayed for them to vanish, and they did for a time, only to re-appear permanently in 1918. His superiors were very suspicious of these phenomena, and for a time forbade him to hear confessions or celebrate Mass. They also had him investigated by sceptical doctors and by the Inquisition. Padre Pio bore all of these humiliations without complaint. Eventually he was allowed to resume his priestly ministry, and devoted himself to hearing confessions, to spiritual direction, and to works of compassion for the sick, founding a hospital. People came in their thousands to make their confession to him, and to join his celebration of Mass. He suffered persistent ill-health, and hardly seemed to need food except the Eucharist. There are many stories of his miraculous interventions in the lives of those who needed his help. He died in 1968, half a century after receiving the stigmata; but the many miracles attributed to his intercession have not ceased. He was canonized in 2002.

First Day: You were physically conformed to Christ's passion, and bore the likeness of his wounds in your own flesh. Help us to see and accept our sufferings as a participation in Christ's sufferings for the salvation of the world. We pray especially for [*add your intention*]. *Our Father - Hail Mary - Glory Be*

Second Day: You accepted persecution and mis-understanding without complaint. Help us to be similarly patient when others do us wrong. We pray especially for [*add your intention*]. *Our Father - Hail Mary - Glory Be*

Third Day: Your witness to Christ was not bounded by time and space; help us to see that God's presence and power in our lives is similarly without limit. We pray especially for [*add your intention*]. *Our Father - Hail Mary - Glory Be*

Fourth Day: You were a man of intense and constant prayer. Help us to have a real love of prayer, and to base all we do on a personal relationship with Jesus Christ. We pray especially for [*add your intention*]. *Our Father - Hail Mary - Glory Be*

Fifth Day: You had a deep compassion for the sick and the suffering. Help us to see the face of Christ especially in those who suffer, and to show them something of the love the Father has for his Son; and to see our own sufferings not as a meaningless burden but as the transforming gift of the

Cross. We pray especially for [*add your intention*]. *Our Father - Hail Mary - Glory Be*

Sixth Day: Your compassion extended particularly to those who despair. Help us not to lose hope, or fall prey to discouragement; and, like you, to be a witness to Christ's enduring love for all God's people. We pray especially for [*add your intention*]. *Our Father - Hail Mary - Glory Be*

Seventh Day: You spent long hours hearing confessions, and brought the sacrament of Christ's reconciling love to countless thousands. Help us never to be afraid to open our sins to the overwhelming mercy of God. We pray especially for [*add your intention*]. *Our Father - Hail Mary - Glory Be*

Eighth Day: You gave a great example of the humble life of a priest; intercede for all priests, and those who may be called to this vocation, that like you they may lead truly holy lives and be living icons of Jesus Christ in love for his people. We pray especially for [*add your intention*]. *Our Father - Hail Mary - Glory Be*

Ninth Day: You celebrated the Eucharist with great faithfulness and devotion. Help us all to have a strong desire to meet Jesus Christ in the Eucharist, and know and love him really present in his Word, in his Body and Blood, and in the Christian assembly. We pray especially for [*add your intention*]. *Our Father - Hail Mary - Glory Be*

Novena to St Joseph of Cupertino

Feast day: September 18th

Because his father had died leaving debts and his family was consequently homeless, Joseph Desa was an unwelcome addition when he was born in Cupertino, Italy in 1603. As a child he was slow witted and had a habit of standing with his mouth open staring into space. He also had a terrible temper, probably born of frustration. Even his own mother thought him worthless. As a young man he joined the Capuchins but was sent away because the ecstasies he experienced made him unsuitable for work. Finally he was accepted by the Franciscans who, seeing his holiness, put him forward to train for the priesthood. Joseph was so unintelligent that the best he could do was to study a small portion of the material he was supposed to know, and then pray that that's what he would be asked. Whilst with the Franciscans he began to levitate in ecstasy at the mention of any holy thing and only a command from his superior could bring him to earth. Joseph was investigated (and exonerated) by the Inquisition because of his antigravitational activities. This also caused his superiors to move him into seclusion. He had his own room and chapel and was unable to leave them. Often those in charge even forgot to bring him food but he accepted everything with humility. He died a holy death aged sixty. He is a patron of students doing exams and of air travellers.

First Day: You were an unwanted child and were thought worthless even by your own mother. Intercede for all unwanted children that they may come to know they were born out of God's love for them. We pray especially for [*add your intention*]. *Our Father - Hail Mary - Glory Be*

Second Day: You were an angry, frustrated child. We pray for all who struggle to express themselves, and that you help us overcome sins of anger. We pray especially for [*add your intention*]. *Our Father - Hail Mary - Glory Be*

Third Day: You experienced no love in your family and were considered of little account by all who knew you. We pray for all who have experienced the same. May we learn to treat everyone as having the worth they have in God's eyes. We pray especially for [*add your intention*]. *Our Father - Hail Mary - Glory Be*

Fourth Day: You suffered because of your lack of intelligence. We pray for all those who struggle at school. May they take comfort from the fact that lack of intelligence didn't stop you becoming a saint. We pray especially for [*add your intention*]. *Our Father - Hail Mary - Glory Be*

Fifth Day: You did the best with the little intelligence you had, and put the rest in God's hands. That way you passed all your exams and became a priest. We pray for all those struggling with exams. May we also do our best in everything and trust in God to guide our lives. We pray especially for [*add your intention*]. *Our Father - Hail Mary - Glory Be*

Sixth Day: Even the thought or mention of anything holy made you levitate in ecstasy. Grant us something of the understanding and reverence for God and his saints that you had. We pray especially for [*add your intention*]. *Our Father - Hail Mary - Glory Be*

Seventh Day: Only when your superior ordered you to, were you able to come back down to earth. May we too have a love for and obedience to the teachings of the Church. We pray especially for [*add your intention*]. *Our Father - Hail Mary - Glory Be*

Eighth Day: You were unjustly suspected, investigated, confined to your room and neglected by those charged with looking after you. You accepted all this with humility. We pray for all those unjustly imprisoned, and that we too may have the humility to accept injustice for the love of Christ. We pray especially for [*add your intention*]. *Our Father - Hail Mary - Glory Be*

Ninth Day: Because you could levitate you are the patron of air travellers. We pray for all those travelling by plane that they may safely reach their destinations. We pray especially for [*add your intention*]. *Our Father - Hail Mary - Glory Be*

Novena to St Raphael

Feast day: September 29th; with St Michael & St Gabriel
(formerly October 24th)

St Raphael's name means, in Hebrew, "God heals". He is first
mentioned in the Book of Tobit, where he is called "one of the
seven who stand before God". The Church has considered him
one of the Archangels, alongside Michael and Gabriel (and
others for whom we have no names). The Book of Tobit is a
great image of Christian marriage, and the Archangel Raphael
plays a central role in it in bringing together the young couple,
Tobias and Sarah, and protecting them from the attempts of the
Devil to destroy their union. He is thus the particular patron of
marriage, of single people looking for a marriage partner, and of
those seeking God's protection against anything that might
threaten their married life. He is also a patron of those
undertaking journeys, particularly long or difficult ones.

First Day: You are known as the Angel of Joy; help us
always to be joyful in God's service, and see His loving
hand in all the events He sends us. We pray especially for
[*add your intention*]. *Our Father - Hail Mary - Glory Be*

Second Day: You are known as the Angel of Healing.
Intercede for all those who need healing of mind or body,
and obtain for them the consolations of God's love. We pray
especially for [*add your intention*]. *Our Father - Hail Mary -
Glory Be*

Third Day: You are known as a powerful protector against demons. Protect us against all the attacks of the Evil One, all his wiles and deceits, especially the lie he tells us that we cannot be loved. We pray especially for [*add your intention*]. *Our Father - Hail Mary - Glory Be*

Fourth Day: You are known as a giver of peace of mind. Help us always to live in that peace God gives to his children, whatever our outward circumstances. We pray especially for [*add your intention*]. *Our Father - Hail Mary - Glory Be*

Fifth Day: You are known as the Angel of Love. Help us to know God's love for us, and be able to have this same love for our neighbour. We particularly ask this grace for married couples, and those discerning a vocation to married life. We pray especially for [*add your intention*]. *Our Father - Hail Mary - Glory Be*

Sixth Day: You are an especial patron of youth, and the angel of happy meetings and wise choices. Help all who are young wisely to discern what God calls them to do, guide them on their path in life, and be with them in all the encounters God sends them. We pray especially for [*add your intention*]. *Our Father - Hail Mary - Glory Be*

Seventh Day: You are called the angel of everyday life. Help us all to see God's hand in our daily lives, even in events that may seem trivial to us, and to see God's loving mercy in them all; help us to make God's love present in our world. We pray especially for [*add your intention*]. *Our Father - Hail Mary - Glory Be*

Eighth Day: You are the patron of travel. Be with all who have journeys to make: protect them on their way, and bring them safely to their destination. We pray especially for [*add your intention*]. *Our Father - Hail Mary - Glory Be*

Ninth Day: You are known as the Angel of Last Anointing, who watch over those called from this life to God. Be with us and protect us when we make our last journey, our great Passover into the eternal country, to God's holy mountain. We pray especially for [*add your intention*]. *Our Father - Hail Mary - Glory Be*

Here are two traditional prayers to St. Raphael for the wise choice of a marriage partner. You could say any one of these over nine days as a novena for this intention.

Traditional prayer to St Raphael

Glorious St Raphael, patron and lover of the young, I call upon you and ask for your help. In all confidence I open my heart to you, to beg your guidance and assistance in the important task of planning my future. Obtain for me through your intercession the light of God's grace, so that I may decide wisely concerning the person who is to be my partner through life. O Angel of Happy Meetings, lead us by the hand to find each other. May all our movements be guided by your light and transfigured by your joy. As you led the young Tobias to Sarah and opened up for him a new life of happiness with her in holy marriage, lead me to the one whom in your angelic wisdom you judge best suited to be united with me in marriage.

Amen

Prayer of an engaged couple

St Raphael, angel of chaste courtship, bless our friendship and our love, that sin may have no part in it. May our mutual love bind us so closely that our future home may always be most like the home of the Holy Family of Nazareth. Offer your prayers to God for both of us, and obtain the blessing of God upon our marriage, just as you were the herald of blessing for the marriage of Tobias and Sarah.

Amen

Novena to St Thérèse of Lisieux

Feast day: October 1st

 Thérèse Martin was born into a bourgeois family in France in 1873. She lost her mother at an early age; this changed her from being a happy child to one who was withdrawn and neurotic. Her close relationship with her father, however, helped her to understand the fatherhood of God. She entered Carmel as an enclosed nun at the age of only fifteen (after badgering the Pope, and getting special permission from her Bishop), and stayed there until she died aged only twenty-three.

Under obedience, she had written a short autobiography; this was later published, and inspired many to follow her "little way" of humble confidence in God. She was proclaimed a Doctor of the Church in 1997.

She always wanted to travel, and to be a missionary, but was unable to do so, apart from one brief trip to Rome. Since her death, however, her relics have travelled the world, and have even been into space. She promised to spend her time in heaven doing good on earth, and her many devotees know she keeps that promise.

First Day: As a small child, you were absolutely obstinate. Intercede for parents whose children are headstrong. Help them to be firm but loving. We pray especially for [*add your intention*]. *Our Father - Hail Mary - Glory Be*

Second Day: You were very close to your father. Help Christian fathers to show their children something of the loving fatherhood of God. We pray especially for [*add your intention*]. *Our Father - Hail Mary - Glory Be*

Third Day: You suffered from being neurotic and scrupulous. Help all those who suffer in this way to know God's love and mercy. We pray especially for [*add your intention*]. *Our Father - Hail Mary - Glory Be*

Fourth Day: You so wanted to enter Carmel you were not afraid to ask the Pope himself, and were ready to endure the humiliation of being removed by the Swiss Guard. Help us not to reject God's will for us because we are afraid of being humiliated. We pray especially for [*add your intention*]. *Our Father - Hail Mary - Glory Be*

Fifth Day: You showed the greatest consideration for those you disliked. Help us to learn not to judge, but to be kind and understanding. We pray especially for [*add your intention*]. *Our Father - Hail Mary - Glory Be*

Sixth Day: You prayed especially for priests. We pray that all who are called may accept their vocation. We ask God to keep his hand on them and protect them. We pray especially for [*add your intention*]. *Our Father - Hail Mary - Glory Be*

Seventh Day: You knew that God is a father who loves us and who keeps his promises. Help us to have that same confidence and assurance. We pray especially for [*add your intention*]. *Our Father - Hail Mary - Glory Be*

Eighth Day: You experienced the pain and suffering of tuberculosis, which was then incurable. We pray for all those who have painful or terminal illnesses. Intercede for them that they may know the comfort of their loving Father. We pray especially for [*add your intention*]. *Our Father - Hail Mary - Glory Be*

Ninth Day: You understood that it is not the apparent greatness or smallness of what we are called to do that is important in God's sight, but, rather, that we do whatever He sends us to do with a loving heart and with generosity of spirit. We pray to have this same understanding. We pray especially for [*add your intention*]. *Our Father - Hail Mary - Glory Be*

Novena Prayer to St Gerard Majella

Feast day: October 16th

Gerard Majella was born near Naples, Italy in 1726. His father was a tailor, and died when Gerard was twelve. Although his mother and uncle wanted him to take up the family business, Gerard was called to the religious life. He was unable to join the Capuchin order because of poor health, but was finally accepted by the Redemptorists as a lay brother when he was twenty-three. He lived only for a short time longer, dying of tuberculosis in 1755, aged twenty-nine. His life was marked by patient acceptance of suffering and injustice. Most famously, he was falsely accused by an unmarried mother of being the father of her child. He made no protest but accepted the judgements of those around him in silence and patience until, eventually, the woman admitted she had lied. For this reason, St Gerard is known as an especial patron of motherhood, of unborn children, and of childbirth. He is often invoked by those who are trying to have children, and by expectant mothers.

Here are two traditional prayers to St Gerard, one for motherhood, and one for safe delivery of a child. Either could be said over nine days as a novena.

Prayer for motherhood

Good St Gerard, powerful intercessor before God and wonderworker of our day, I call on you and seek your aid. You, who on earth always fulfilled God's design, help me to do God's holy will. Beseech the master of life, from whom all parenthood comes, to make me fruitful, so I may raise up children to God in this life and heirs to the kingdom of his glory in the world to come.

Amen

Prayer for safe delivery

Great St Gerard, beloved servant of Jesus Christ, perfect imitator of your meek and humble Saviour, and devoted child of the Mother of God: enkindle within my heart a spark of that heavenly fire of charity that glowed in yours, and made you a seraph of love.

Glorious St Gerard, because when you were falsely accused of crime, you bore like your Divine Master without murmur or complaint the calumnies of wicked men, you have been raised up by God as patron and protector of expectant mothers. Preserve me from danger and from the excessive pains accompanying childbirth, and shield the child which I now carry, that it may see the light of day and receive the cleansing waters of baptism; through Christ our Lord.

Amen

Novena to St Jude

Feast day: October 28th

The apostle St Jude takes only a modest role in the Gospel narratives, but he is probably the best-known intercessor of all the Twelve. According to tradition, St Jude, together with his companion the apostle St Simon (not Simon Peter, but Simon the Zealot) who may have been his brother, preached the Gospel in various parts of the middle east (Persia, Mesopotamia, Armenia, and around the Black Sea) and were eventually martyred in Georgia.

For some reason, St Jude has become known as the saint of lost causes, or of things despaired of: someone whose intercession is especially powerful in cases where all hope seems gone. Whatever the reason for this, many people can testify to the strength of his prayers for them.

First Day: O blessed apostle, St Jude, who laboured among the peoples of many lands and performed miracles in despairing cases, I ask you to take an interest in my need. You understand me. Hear my prayer, and plead for me. May I be patient in learning God's will and courageous in carrying it out. We pray especially for [*add your intention*]. *Our Father - Hail Mary - Glory Be*

Second Day: O blessed apostle, St Jude, grant that I may always serve the Lord as he deserves to be served, and live as he wants me to live. I ask you to intercede for me. May I be enlightened as to what is best for me now, and not forget the blessings I have received in the past. We pray especially for [*add your intention*]. *Our Father - Hail Mary - Glory Be*

Third Day: Holy St Jude, who so faithfully helped to spread the Gospel, I ask you to remember me and my needs. May the Lord listen to your prayers on my behalf. May I always pray with fervour and devotion, resigning myself to God's will, and seeing his purposes in all my trials. Help me to know that God will not leave any sincere prayer unanswered. We pray especially for [*add your intention*]. *Our Father - Hail Mary - Glory Be*

Fourth Day: St Jude, you were called as one of the apostles. Listen with compassion as I ask for your help; pray that God may answer my prayer as he knows best, giving me grace to see his purpose in all things. We pray especially for [*add your intention*]. *Our Father - Hail Mary - Glory Be*

Fifth Day: Holy St Jude, apostle and companion of Jesus Christ, your life was filled with zeal for the Gospel. Listen to my prayers now. May I never forget the blessings I have received in the past, and may I be resigned to God's holy will. We pray especially for [*add your intention*]. *Our Father - Hail Mary - Glory Be*

Sixth Day: St Jude, apostle of Christ and helper in desperate cases, listen to my prayer. May I seek only what pleases God and is best for my salvation. May what I desire be granted, if it is for my good; help me to know that God leaves no prayer without an answer, even if it is not what I may expect. We pray especially for [*add your intention*]. *Our Father - Hail Mary - Glory Be*

Seventh Day: Holy apostle, St Jude, Christ chose you as one of the Twelve, and you were given the gift of martyrdom. I know you are close to God. Listen to my request; and help me to see God's purpose in all things. We pray especially for [*add your intention*]. *Our Father - Hail Mary - Glory Be*

Eighth Day: Holy St Jude, pray that I may always imitate Christ and live according to his will. Intercede for me, that I may obtain whatever I need for my salvation. Help me to accept from God whatever answer he gives to what I now ask. We pray especially for [*add your intention*]. *Our Father - Hail Mary - Glory Be*

Ninth Day: Holy St Jude, apostle and martyr, help my life be pleasing to God. Intercede for me today; pray especially that I may seek God's will above all things, and see his love for me in whatever trials or difficulties he sends me. We pray especially for [*add your intention*]. *Our Father - Hail Mary - Glory Be*

Novena to St Martin de Porres

Feast day: November 3rd

Martin was born in Peru in 1579, the illegitimate son of a Spanish father and a mother who was a freed slave. Rejected by his father for being too black, he grew up in poverty with his mother and sister. From an early age he had a great love of God and of the poor. He became a Dominican lay brother as he could not be accepted into the order because of his colour. He worked in menial jobs and then as an infirmarian. He became renowned for his medical ability but he eschewed the fame that came with that and remained humble and hidden. He was also known for his love of the poor and also of animals, especially dogs. He was canonized in 1962 and is the patron of interracial harmony.

First Day: You were rejected and abandoned by your father. We pray for all those who experience that same situation and for all those who are rejected for not meeting their family's expectations in some way. May they be reconciled, as you were finally reconciled with your own father. We pray especially for [*add your intention*]. *Our Father - Hail Mary - Glory Be*

Second Day: As a child your mother was your only parent. We pray for all single parent families, and ask that you help them in the particular difficulties that they face. We pray especially for [*add your intention*]. *Our Father - Hail Mary - Glory Be*.

Third Day: You grew up poor but you always gave to those who had even less. We ask you to help us to become generous with our goods and our time, never feeling that we have nothing to offer. We pray especially for [*add your intention*]. *Our Father - Hail Mary - Glory Be*

Fourth Day: When you were eight your father reappeared and whisked you off to a prosperous life in another country before sending you back to the life you had before. We pray for all those whose family life is insecure and disrupted. May they experience, as you did, that God is their security. We pray especially for [*add your intention*]. *Our Father - Hail Mary - Glory Be*

Fifth Day: You lived alone working to support yourself from a very young age. We pray for all children who have adult responsibilities; for all children who support their families; and for all children who are carers for their parents. Intercede for them that they may receive the help they need. We pray especially for [*add your intention*]. *Our Father - Hail Mary - Glory Be*

Sixth Day: You were rejected because of your colour - even by the church. We pray for all those who suffer discrimination of any kind. May all in authority deal with everyone justly, and may we treat each other as brothers and sisters in Christ. We pray especially for [*add your intention*]. *Our Father - Hail Mary - Glory Be*

Seventh Day: You were not ashamed to do the most menial of jobs. You were even happy cleaning lavatories. May we too learn humility and come to see that all work can be holy. We pray especially for [*add your intention*]. *Our Father - Hail Mary - Glory Be*

Eighth Day: You were known for your love of animals. Help us to love and respect all God's creation. We pray especially for [*add your intention*]. *Our Father - Hail Mary - Glory Be*

Ninth Day: You had great medical skill and love for other people. We pray for all who are involved in caring for the sick. May they share something of your compassion and your skill. We pray especially for [*add your intention*]. *Our Father - Hail Mary - Glory Be.*

Novena Prayer to St Andrew

Feast day: November 30th

The Apostle St Andrew, brother to Simon Peter, has been invoked as intercessor and patron since the early years of the Church. After the Resurrection, according to legend he preached the Gospel in Scythia (north of the Black Sea), in Asia Minor, and in Greece. He is traditionally said to have been martyred in Patras on the gulf of Corinth, crucified on a "saltire" cross (hence the well-known flag of St Andrew); relics of him are still found there, and also in many other places, including, at one time, St Andrew's in Scotland. As well as being Scotland's patron, he is also patron of Greece, Russia, the Ukraine, Romania and various European towns and cities.

Novena Prayer to St Andrew

St Andrew, you were the first to recognize and follow the Lamb of God. With your friend, St John, you remained with Jesus for that first day, for your entire life, and now throughout eternity. As you led your brother St Peter to Christ and many others after him, draw us also to Him. Teach us to lead others to Christ solely out of love for Him and dedication to His service. Help us to learn the lesson of the Cross and to carry our daily crosses without complaint so that they may carry us to Jesus.

Amen

Novena to Blessed Charles de Foucauld

Feast day: December 1st

 As a young man, Charles de Foucauld was rich and privileged. He ran through a small fortune on high living and mistresses, and sought adventure in the army and in exotic travel. Eventually, God touched his heart, and he gave up his old life to enter a monastery. But this was not enough for him; he returned to the deserts of North Africa, where as a young soldier he had been impressed by the religious devotion of the Muslim tribesmen, and lived amongst them as a hermit, witnessing to Christ without words, but simply by his way of life. He was shot to death by robbers in 1916, when after fifteen years in the desert he had made only one convert. But, despite appearances, his life and witness was not in vain: after his death, his example has brought many to God, and inspires the "Little Brothers and Sisters of Jesus", who follow Charles's example by living in "the lowest place", and seek to bring God's love to others in a silent and hidden way.

First Day: You knew what it is like to be burdened by many sins. Help us not to despair in the face of our sins, especially our habitual sins, but really to believe in God's power to change us. We pray especially for [*add your intention*]. *Our Father - Hail Mary - Glory Be*

Second Day: You turned to God, and knew his mercy on your sins. Help us to hear his call to repent the evil we have done, and to welcome the grace to return to our loving

Father as you did. We pray especially for [*add your intention*].
Our Father - Hail Mary - Glory Be

Third Day: You heard God's to follow him in a particular
way. Help us, too, to hear God's call to us to love him and
our neighbour in the vocation he has planned for us. We
pray especially for [*add your intention*]. *Our Father - Hail
Mary - Glory Be*

Fourth Day: You lived amongst strangers, and saw God's
hand at work in them. Help us to find God wherever we are,
especially in the places we might not think to look for him.
We pray especially for [*add your intention*]. *Our Father - Hail
Mary - Glory Be*

Fifth Day: You lived in the desert, and found God in
solitude and silence. Help us to make space for God in our
lives. We pray especially for [*add your intention*]. *Our Father -
Hail Mary - Glory Be*

Sixth Day: You gave witness to God most of all by what
you did, rather than by what you said. Pray for us, that we
too may be a sign of God's love to those around us, more by
how we live than by what we say. We pray especially for
[*add your intention*]. *Our Father - Hail Mary - Glory Be*

Seventh Day: Your mission seemed to be a failure, and your life's work to have come to nothing, yet you did not give up. Help us to persevere in doing God's will, even if – especially if – we can see only failure and defeat: help us to know that, in God's sight, the only important thing is to do his will in love, and to live in hope, not discouragement. We pray especially for [*add your intention*]. *Our Father - Hail Mary - Glory Be*

Eighth Day: You abandoned your whole life to God's will. Pray for us, that we may have something of the faith you had. We pray especially for [*add your intention*]. *Our Father - Hail Mary - Glory Be*

Ninth Day: You loved God until the end, and even in your death you praised him. Intercede for us, that death may find us blessing God for all his mercies. We pray especially for [*add your intention*]. *Our Father - Hail Mary - Glory Be*